Economic Management in China

Joan Robinson

Anglo-Chinese Educational Institute
1975

Contents

Foreword to First Edition

These notes can offer no more than a scrappy and impressionistic account of the system of planning and management which is evolving in China in the 'period of transformation' emerging from 'the struggle and criticism' of the Cultural Revolution.

Thanks to the great generosity of the Chinese People's Association for Friendship with Foreign Countries, I was able to travel in China for six weeks in the spring of 1972, visiting Peking, Shenyang, Wuhan, Nanking, Shanghai and Canton, with a number of excursions into the surrounding districts. I received reports and held discussions with members of the administrations of provinces, enterprises, counties, communes and neighbourhoods. Many busy people gave me and my companions a great deal of time and patiently answered my often ignorant questions. I was able to learn far more than I have found out by reading or visits before. All the same, my information is slight and superficial. It applies only to the particular places that I visited. No doubt there are many differences in other regions and other institutions. I was fortunate in having an excellent and careful interpreter, but obviously it is a drawback not to be able to understand for oneself. I hope that the questions that I was able to open will inspire more adequate investigation by others who have the language and the background that I lack.

Cambridge, July 1972.

Second edition

The text of the first edition has been amended at a few points, and a Postscript added, with the aid of Roland Berger and other friends at the Society for Anglo-Chinese Understanding.

Cambridge, August 1974.

Joan Robinson

1. For use, not for profit

One element in the 'struggle between two lines' which burst into turmoil during the Cultural Revolution was the problem of motivation for work in a socialist economy. How far must the system appeal to individual interests and how far can it rely on revolutionary spirit? After violent swings to right and left, now, in the 'period of transformation' a new balance is being established.

In China, work is organised in three main forms, under state ownership of the means of production, agricultural Communes with collective ownership of land and of the proceeds of their own accumulation, and collective enterprises in small-scale industry, some of which are now growing quite large. Each form has its own balance between material and moral incentives to maintain production.

Industry

Wage rates and bonuses

In China now, as far as the state sector is concerned, that is to say the whole of regular industry and commerce, a clean sweep has been made of all individual payment by results. A group bonus to an enterprise as a whole, distributed to the workers, is not unknown but to dispense with this kind of incentive for improved production is held to show a higher level of political consciousness. Formerly there was a system of personal bonuses, copied from the Soviet Union; during the Cultural Revolution this was abolished at the demand of the workers. The workers said: It is true that some get more money income with bonuses, but then others get less. The system was so complicated that no one could work out what was due to him, and anyway the whole conception seemed to them insulting, particularly special bonuses for what everyone should regard as his duty, such as care in avoiding accidents. They objected also to group bonuses which went to the welfare fund of individual enterprises. If the welfare fund is necessary, it ought to be assured. Now there is simply the national scale of wage rates, no piece rates or overtime pay and the welfare fund of each enterprise is a regular proportion of its wage bill (generally 11 per cent) which is reckoned as part of the cost of production of output.

There is a nation-wide system of wage grades at three levels. There are eight steps for workers from 33 to 108 yuan a month; a 15-grade system for technicians and a 25-grade system for cadres. As an example, in a Kwangchow factory the worker receiving the highest pay was in the seventh grade with carried 100 yuan a month, the lowest in the second grade at 45 yuan. Here the highest-paid technician received 96 yuan a month (tenth grade) and the leading cadres 135 yuan (fifteenth grade). There are lower rates for apprentices and a higher rate is sometimes allowed in special circumstances.

An individual's grade depends upon length of service, skill and 'political attitude', that is, diligence, unselfishness, helpfulness, willingness to take on the awkward jobs and so forth. There is evidently a certain negative monetary incentive in the desire not to miss promotion to a higher grade, but it seems that promotion in the ordinary way is more or less automatic at least over the lower grades. During the Cultural Revolution due promotions were forgotten; in August 1971 there was a ruling that, over the lower grades, promotions were to be made on a regular plan. Workers in the third grade or below who had been at work before 1957 must be raised to the fourth grade; those in the second grade who had been at work before 1960 should be raised to the third grade, and those in the first grade who were at work before 1966 should be raised to the second. The period of work of an apprentice counted towards his promotion and so did a period of service in the army.

The additional pay had to be back-dated to July 1971, so that individual workers would not suffer by delay in an enterprise that took a long time to work it out. A delay of nine or ten months made quite a lump of new purchasing power and caused a spurt of demand, when it came, for such things as bicycles and sewing machines, but supplies were available so that this injection of purchasing power had no inflationary effect.

Apprentices (like students) get an allowance which enables them to live (often in dormitories provided by the enterprise) with not more than 6 yuan a month of pocket money — but clothes are provided.

Arguments in favour of virtually abolishing differentials altogether came up during the Cultural Revolution. For the time being these have been dismissed as ultra-left. On the other hand, the recent promotions for lower-grade workers required some 'political education' of workers in the top grades who got no benefit from it.

There are no longer any bonuses to individual workers for inventions or technical improvements, but the encouragement to initiative is stronger than before. Whenever snags appear or whenever a worker has a bright idea, a triple unit of workers, technicians and cadres concerned with management is set to work to solve problems or improve design and operation of equipment.

There are no bonuses for managers as there are in the Soviet system and no pecuniary advantages from success to an enterprise as a whole, such as extra payments to the welfare fund as a reward for output in excess of the plan. The management of an enterprise has been allotted a certain number of workers, technicians and cadres and receives the appropriate wage fund. Prices of materials and products are all given in the plan. Prices include a proportion of profits. Good management, economy and high output per head increase the total profit. Total profit is handed over to the state (that is, to the city or province where the enterprise is situated) without distinction between planned and over-planned profit. A failure to achieve planned profit, unless for some acceptable reason, obviously would cause the management to be criticised, but it does not directly affect anyone's personal income.

Prices and profit margins

It seems that the movement since the Cultural Revolution in China is in the exact opposite direction from the economic reforms in the Soviet sphere. The tendency of the proposals associated with the name of Liberman, of the abortive reforms of Ota Sik and of some actual methods in use in Hungary, is based on the conception of giving more independence and financial responsibility to the management of the individual enterprise and using profitability of production as the criterion of success. The claim for these schemes is that they improve efficiency by breaking out of the rigidity and over-centralisation of Soviet-style planning.

Breaking out of that system can no doubt produce striking immediate improvements, but 'market socialism' seems to run into a fundamental objection, quite apart from the erosion of socialist morality that monetary incentives bring about. The difficulty is connected with the determination of prices. When the enterprise has the right to fix the prices of its own products, much of the waste and irrationality, such as is only too familiar to us in a market economy, is bound to follow — monopolistic prices, advertisement, catering to tastes of the higher income families and neglecting the needs of the poorer ones. In Yugoslavia, giving the workers of each enterprise a direct interest in its profits worked wonders as far as the internal efficiency of management was concerned but it failed to give them an interest in providing employment for others or in evening up the level of development between regions. Moreover, it gives them the same interest as capitalist firms have in pricing their goods on the principle of charging what the traffic will bear.

The Chinese regard 'putting profits in command' as 'taking the capitalist road'. In so far as the profit criterion was used, under the influence of Liu Shao-chi, it led to anomalies. (Here, of course, profit does not mean the expected rate of return on investment, but an allowance for a margin of profit in the final price of products.) Enterprises were not allowed to fix their own prices, but so long as they had an interest in the level of earnings and were instructed to maximise profits, the composition of output for an enterprise was influenced by the relative rates of profit (which correspond to the mark-up on direct costs in capitalist industry) for different items rather than by the composition of demand — say demand from the communes for small rather than heavy tractors or from households for children's clothes rather than grown-up sizes. It is impossible to work out such a delicate system of profit ratios as to get exactly the desirable product mix. A policy of going forward from the system in force before the Cultural Revolution towards putting the market in complete command (as under the proposals of Ota Sik) was rejected in the 'struggle against revisionism'.

Under the system now in force, the prices of all outputs and inputs are given to the enterprise; its plan of production is worked out in consultation with higher authorities; carrying it out depends on self-respect and public spirit or, as the Chinese put it, on the high level of political consciousness of the workers. (The principles on which prices are set is discussed below.)

Consumer demand

The Chinese system avoids the problem which is tormenting the planners in the Soviet sphere; that is, how to make use of their now considerable industrial productive capacity to supply consumers with consumption goods that they actually want to consume. So long as initiative and economic power lie with the producer, the enterprises are accustomed to produce what suits them and throw it on to the market whether the public want it or not. Now that the Soviet Union has arrived at potential affluence, they are at a loss to know how to make use of it.

To devise a system that takes account of the consumer's needs and tastes, China did not wait for potential affluence.

Representatives of the Department of Commerce, who are in charge of retailing, provide the services of a wholesaler at every level. They are concerned in the process of planning for light industry and so can influence the composition of output to fit the consumer's preferences reported from the shops, and they keep a finger on the pulse of the overall relation of demand to supply so that when output has expanded relatively to total expenditure, some prices can be cut. The prices chosen to be cut is a matter of policy — recently the chief benefit has gone to medicines, which were selling in 1972 at 20 per cent of the prices ruling in 1950. (So long as industry yields profit to the state over all, it does not matter that some commodities are sold at a loss.)

The shops take trouble to serve consumer needs; pharmacies provide first-aid for simple cases; in the city, when the night shift from a big factory comes off at 1 am, local shops are open; there are all-night bicycle repair shops in Peking; in the country, the village shop (still formally a 'supply and marketing co-operative', but actually supplied by the commerce department) sends shoulder-loads of goods up to the mountains when commune members are camping beside their work.

The system of controlling light industry through wholesaling began when the 'national capitalists' in the coastal cities were instructed to continue producing after Liberation. They were supplied with raw materials and given contracts to produce finished goods, mainly textiles. By the end of 1956 all had been absorbed into the state-private system and had come fully into the sphere of the planned economy.

The method of operating through contracts is still widely used. For instance, the department of commerce of a city makes contracts for fruit and vegetables with surrounding communes. The deal is made in overall wholesale terms between the city and the commune, and then broken down into detailed day-by-day deliveries from each particular team to each shop or street-side stall.

Formerly, say, tomatoes had a short season and were dumped on to the public all at once. ('We used to think,' said a commune spokesman, 'what we produce, they have to eat.') Now, production is staggered out over as long a season as possible (a 'greenhouse' is used which consists of a sheet of plastic stretched between two banks of earth). With cold storage, apples are on sale all over the country all the year round.

Manufactured consumer goods are also dealt with by means of contracts. The contract, say for a textile factory, with the department of commerce, specifies design, quality and delivery dates for three months' output. The weaver, in turn, has a contract for supplies of yarns and so forth. The finished goods are allocated to particular shops. An enterprise that fails to fulfil its contract has to compensate the purchaser, generally by making up the deficiency later.

In some provinces, operating through contracts has been superseded by what is regarded as a more satisfactory method. The department of commerce, say of a city, knows the planned output of the local factories, and it knows what has been allocated for local consumption; it has had a hand in framing and agreeing the plan. The staff of the department is divided into companies concerned with different groups of commodities; the companies purchase the planned quantities of the various commodities (balancing overfulfilment with deficiency, or adjusting the plan as required) and pass the goods to the shops.

There has been a great drive to diversify local production to make each area as self-sufficient as possible. The city of Shenyang in the North East, a highly specialised centre of heavy industry, formerly imported from outside its municipal boundary 70 per cent of its agricultural and manufactured consumer goods. During the Cultural Revolution, mainly by mobilising women as workers and by encouraging suburban communes to diversify production, they reversed the proportions and now provide 70 per cent for themselves.

It is not only through the operation of the Department of Commerce that Chinese planning establishes consumer's sovereignty over supplies. The individual enterprises also concern themselves to cater to the tastes of the public. The enterprise gets information from the shops directly about customers' opinions and sends some workers and cadres to serve behind the counter where its products are being sold. It encourages the public to write in their complaints and suggestions. It sends workers into the country and to the army to ask about requirements. One instance that was quoted was that when villagers complained that the rubber boots they were getting had treads too shallow for wearing in the mud, the enterprise concerned got hold of an old heavy nailed boot and used it as a model.

Enterprises in the same line exchange designs with each other and they collect samples from abroad. Since the public can only choose between what already exists, it is up to the enterprise to carry out research (for instance, a textile factory is working on the properties of synthetic fibres) and try out new designs. From time to time there is an exhibition sale of newly produced goods in a department store.

The general principle of this system is that the workers and the management of an enterprise are concerned with efficiency and quality of production, but have nothing to do with sales.

Export corporations

The export corporations operate independently of the Department of Commerce. They select particular factories to send samples to the twice-yearly Kwangchow Export Fair and place contracts according to the foreign orders received. Only the best quality products are offered for export. When I remarked to the manager of a factory who had got orders from the Fair, that there must be a contradiction between the demand for exports and home supplies, he said 'Yes, but it is not an antagonistic contradiction.' He could not say himself how the contradiction is resolved: 'They work it out at a higher level'. There is obviously some push and pull between the corporations and the department for supplies. They have to work it out somehow and give the orders to the producers. Exports (and foreign aid) are a sacrifice for the population for there are very few items of which the home market could not absorb more if they were available.

Consumer sovereignity

I have often discussed this problem of consumer sovereignty under socialism with economists from Eastern Europe. I find that they cannot conceive how the Chinese system could work. Certainly, it is a necessary condition for such a system that individuals have no pecuniary interest in production, for as long as income or bonuses depend on sales, there is an irresistible temptation for the producer and the retailer to fix up schemes to exploit the public and share the swag. The Chinese system depends upon a high level of morality (or 'political consciousness') in every sphere from top to bottom. If this has been lost in Eastern Europe, it cannot be recovered merely by changing the relations between commerce and industry. But the Chinese communists are not at all sentimental; they do not rely on morality alone. They rely on the fact that the mass of the workers, who in the nature of the case have nothing to gain from corruption, can see what is going on and, especially since the Cultural Revolution, are alerted to their rights and their duty to keep it clean.

Agriculture

Wage rates and the workpoint system

In agriculture, for the individual, or rather the family, economic incentives are still strong, but they operate at the collective level as well as individually; the individual's share in the income of his group depends on the number of workpoints to his credit, while the value of the workpoint, in kind and in cash, depends on the production of the group. The main structure of the commune has not been changed. Each is divided into brigades, and brigades into teams. The team — workers from round about 50 neighbouring households — is generally the basic accounting unit. There are some brigades which were successful as co-operatives from 1956 or before and now carry on as collective units; I came across one case where the whole commune was the accounting unit; this was an historical accident; one large co-operative, which refused to split up, was created in 1956 and the commune was formed in 1958 by accretion around it.

Various systems of workpoints are in use; sometimes different teams in the same commune use different systems, according to the level of political development that they have reached. The most approved system is used in the famous brigade of Tachai. Everyone has a record kept simply by the half-day worked; at a single annual reckoning, everyone first proposes his own rating, and after discussion, each is awarded marks by his companions, from 10 to 6. The number of days worked is then multiplied by his mark and so his total points allotted. Some teams use the Tachai system but with the difference that the adjudgment of marks is made quarterly or monthly.

A modified Tachai system is the 'pace setter'. In each team, one member is chosen for 10 marks and the rest judge themselves in relation to his performance. Before the Cultural Revolution mainly strength and hard work were taken into account; now there is more stress on 'political attitude'.

Another method is to allot marks in advance to individuals and require the team to reassess them at the end of each month according to how they have done.

The old system, a kind of job evaluation, is still in use in some areas. A points-price is set on each task, say so much for weeding a mou of paddy, so much for picking ten catties of cotton. The task may be given to a group, the group then distribute the points amongst its members; or it may be given to an individual. The proper weight for various jobs may have been a subject of dispute, but after long experience it can be satisfactorily settled.

The advanced communes use a points-price for special jobs, such as building or driving carts. These work out as slightly more remunerative than ordinary agricultural tasks. Moreover, when jobs are being allotted to team members, the most exacting have to be given to the best workers, who have the highest marks. Thus there is some element of job evaluation even in the most advanced system.

The fact that the income received for a workpoint depends on the produce that a team gets from its own particular area of land prevents a negative response of work forthcoming to rising income. Most people, if they are free to choose, prefer to do less work as earnings per unit of effort rise. With the workpoint system, slacking by any individual is doing wrong to his neighbours by checking the rise in the value of the workpoints that all will get. The individual is not free to please himself; he is kept up to the mark by his neighbours. This is another way in which Chinese institutions have been devised to support political motivation instead of pulling against it. Peasants are taught to feel that they are working for the nation, for the Revolution and for all the oppressed people of the world, but they are clearly and obviously doing good for themselves at the same time.

Households — family income and private plots

Scoring workpoints is strictly individual but the basic earning unit in the communes is the family. Generally three generations are living together and often several brothers, with their wives, are sharing a house and pooling their income. Old people who have no family to look after them are given the five guarantees — food, clothing, housing (often in a special home for the aged), medical care and a decent funeral — on the collective welfare fund.

The first claim in a team's output is the grain ration for the households. At the annual reckoning, grain received over the year is set off against the individual's share in distributed income and the balance paid in cash. The team sells its allotted quota of grain to the state; crops such as vegetables, cotton and tobacco are sold for cash. With four or five earners in a household, there is a margin of money income to buy, say, furniture one year and a bicycle the next or to save up to have a house built.

The family also may have a small vegetable garden, a place to keep a pig or a sheep and some chickens, and a private plot to grow grain. The Liu Shao-chi line was to boost the household economy at the expense of the collective and in the fight against his policy there were some who advocated giving up private plots altogether, in emulation of Tachai, but the general view now is that they are useful and should be kept though not enlarged.

At one commune that had done a heroic job of converting a dismal, saline swampy area into well-drained high-yielding paddy land, the secretary of the Party had carried out a campaign for four bigs against four smalls, after the socialist education movement in the countryside which preceded the Cultural Revolution. The four smalls were allowing households to reclaim scraps of land for themselves, adding to the private plots, dividing teams into smaller units, and allowing sales in the free market without control. The four bigs were large-scale pig raising, large-scale fish breeding, forestry and land reclamation. The four bigs have triumphed and raised prosperity all round. The private plots in the paddy fields are now cultivated collectively and each household given the grain, which seems rather like a transitional stage to abolishing the plots altogether, but this seems to be an exceptional case. To advocate getting rid of private plots is now condemned as ultra-left. I even heard a rumour that Tachai (where they were long since abolished) was thinking of re-introducing them so that the householders can have more room to keep chickens.

When a girl marries, the equivalent of her plot is transferred to her husband's household. The total area devoted to private plots is not allowed to increase. I could not find anyone to tell me what is supposed to happen when children grow up.

The local markets

The local markets, which were heavily attacked during the struggle against the Liu line, have come back into vogue in many places. Their scope is limited. It is forbidden to deal in produce that comes under the state plan — grain, oil seeds, cotton, etc. — it is forbidden to buy for re-sale and there is a ceiling to every price. Under the ceiling, prices are settled by supply and demand. Households can sell their private produce and handicrafts and teams may sell fruit and vegetables outside their regular contracts. The markets are strictly controlled and persistent breach of the rules is a criminal offence.

Mechanisation

The commune and the brigades provide a great many services for households and teams, such as ploughing with tractors, threshing and milling grain. For this they charge fees, which contribute to an accumulation fund. At present the main drive is towards mechanisation. The former county machine stations have been wound up and the tractors put at the disposal of communes.

Brigades are now buying tractors with their own funds. There have been difficulties in designing an efficient rice-transplanter. What is described as a semi-mechanised transplanter is being used increasingly in the paddy fields and improved in line with suggestions from the peasants, and field experiments are continuing with fully mechanised types. There is an enormous mass of accumulation required but with better harvests and increased income from sideline occupations, communes and brigades are accumulating funds to buy the equipment they need, which in turn increases productivity. At the same time State assistance to the rural areas has been increasing.*

As well as large-scale state industry, there is a growth in small repair and assembly works, each making a contribution to the huge task; but it will be a long time before the buffalo and the ox finally become redundant.

There is generally a system of three levels for repair and maintenance of equipment. The brigade workshop can do minor repairs; more serious problems are dealt with by the commune, and the county factory can make a thorough overhaul, produce replacements of spare parts and adapt the models provided by regular industry to local requirements. Almost every county in the whole country now has a repair shop of this kind.

---

* According to the People's Daily (January 12, 1974) annual State appropriations for agriculture were then nearly 50 per cent above the 1965 figure.

Foreigners sometimes ask: What is the point of mechanising when the ratio of labour to land is so high? It is true that, in a market economy, mechanisation causes unemployment and reduces the peasantry to misery. This is because the machines are owned by capitalists or kulaks and displace tenants or wage-labourers. The case is quite different when the peasants, collectively, own the machines themselves. First of all, there is often a shortage of labour at peak periods. Secondly, mechanisation often increases total output, as well as output per head, particularly by speeding up cultivation and harvesting, but even if it did not, if it merely reduces back-breaking toil, what is wrong with it? If the peasants want to use their savings in common to make work easier, why should they not? As for 'saving labour', there are plenty of other jobs to be done, diversifying output and setting up small-scale industries as the labour-time required for the main crops is reduced.

As a national policy, the drive for mechanisation is a contribution to increasing the attractiveness of rural life to the younger generation and checking the drift into cities.

Little industries on the communes are springing up every year. Once some peasants have had a few months' training in a factory and have got hold of a couple of obsolete lathes, they seem to be able to set about making equipment for themselves.

One of the most important services that the communes provide for their members is housebuilding. Many have their own brick and tile works. A brigade runs a building team which works continuously dealing with applications from members' families. Some are requests for new dwellings and some are replacing mud with brick. The family usually saves up to pay, but where there is the security of two full-time workers, they may get a loan for part of the price for a year or two. The builders earn workpoints and the money is paid to the brigade. Most workers in commune factories are paid wages. Those at the brigade level earn workpoints; they are generally doing agricultural work during the rush seasons. The general principle is that industrial earnings should be a little, but not much, higher than the average.

The cadres at the commune level are paid salaries by the state; the rest earn workpoints. They have an allowance for time spent at meetings, subject to the rule that it must not absorb more than 2 per cent of a team's income.

Cadres are expected to put in at least 50 days a year in farm work and many do a good deal more. They must be supervised both from above and below, stated the 23 points, but 'The most important supervision is that which comes from the masses.'*

---

* The 23 points, entitled 'Some problems currently arising in the course of the rural socialist education movement' were issued in January 1965.

Small collectives

There are small-scale collective enterprises also outside communes. Some were formed from co-operatives of old handicraftsmen; some were started by housewives in the cities, many of which are now producing sophisticated components for state industry.

The 'five small industries', which are being encouraged to develop whenever they can in the rural areas, are largely in the form of collectives while some are in the form of state enterprises under local control outside the orbit of the national plan. In fact there are more than five. There are small mines for coal and other minerals, small hydro-electric stations and cement works where natural resources permit; small factories producing iron and steel, chemical fertilisers and farm machinery, including spare parts for vehicles of various kinds. All these are growing rapidly. Small-scale cement works, mainly established since 1970, are now producing 40 per cent of total supply; there is a similar situation for chemical fertiliser. A fertiliser plant that started with a capacity of 800 tons a year at the time of the Great Leap in 1958 was producing 2,500 tons ten years later and was in course of expanding, in the spring of 1972, to a capacity of more than 9,000 tons. In the south there is a flourishing industry of building cement boats for the waterways. (The wire netting for the frame is woven on converted automatic looms.)

The collectives sell their products to communes, factories or the local commerce department. The wage they can pay depends on the value of their output. At the same time selling prices are related to costs, which consists largely of wages. It is not clear how the level of wages was set in the first place. It is generally lower than in regular industry but it provides higher earnings than the average in agriculture. The collectives keep about half their profits to provide an accumulation fund. There is no doubt an economic motive for earning wages but pride in achievement is a strong motive too.

The balance of interchange

The basic characteristic of the Chinese economy is that 80 per cent and more of the population, organised in communes, is responsible for feeding and housing itself. The surplus provided by the communes feeds the rest of the population and provides raw materials (particularly cotton) to industry.

The rest of the economy acquires the surplus from agriculture in four ways, from the agriculture tax, quota sales of crops, above quota sales and through the free market. (There are also state farms which are organised on the same basis as industry. I did not have an opportunity to get information about them but I had the impression that, considering how lavishly they are mechanised, they do not compare favourably with the most progressive communes.)

The agricultural tax was instituted after the land reform, while cultivation was in the hands of private peasants. It was assessed on the basis of the normal productivity of each mou of land, amounting at that time to about 14 per cent of gross output. When co-operatives and communes were formed, the liability to tax went with the land; the liability was converted, for cash crops, into money payments equivalent to the value of the grain in the original assessment. A proportion or the whole of the tax is remitted in case of crop failures due to 'natural calamities'. As output per mou has grown, the proportion of tax has automatically fallen; it is now said to be about 6 per cent of gross output on the average of the country as a whole; in some provinces it is about 4 per cent and in particular districts less than 2 per cent.

In some areas, the original assessment, made in 1953, is still in force; in others reassessments were made in 1961 or 1964. The method of reassessment was explained to me in a county near Shanghai where some communes were enjoying a much higher level of income than the average because they were selling vegetables to the city. The overall tax rate was reckoned to be 7.7 per cent at the time that the change was made. Each brigade reported its average income over the past three years. Money income was reduced to the equivalent in grain. Then 7.7 per cent of the notional quantity of grain was taken and divided by the area of cultivable land of the brigades. This gave the tax assessment per mou in terms of grain, to be paid in money at the standard price of grain.

The burden of tax is still uneven between teams and between communes. There seems to have been a directive in 1971 to readjust the tax burden while leaving the total payment for each county unchanged. In one county that I visited, the readjustment had been made, taking progressive proportions of income per head in each team. In other provinces, nothing seemed to be known about it. Some provinces count only 80 per cent of the tax revenue as a contribution to provincial income, so as to leave a margin for meeting remissions.

In some provinces, there is a surcharge of 12 per cent or 16 per cent of the agricultural tax which goes to the county. In others, the county keeps 5 per cent of the tax, in others again the county passes on the whole tax to the province.

The agricultural tax provides less than 10 per cent of national revenue and it might be argued that all this fuss and complication is not worth while, but for the teams in the ordinary run of communes, delivering the tax grain after the harvest has become symbolic; it is made the occasion of a festival, with drums and flags.

The main source of the deliveries from the communes to the rest of the economy, far and away more important than the others, is quota sales. Sales are made at fixed prices, which have been raised from time to time but never lowered. Each team or brigade agrees its annual production plan and its quota of sales. Formerly the quota was related to average output of the last three years; during the Cultural Revolution, the recalculations were not made everywhere. In 1971 a set of quotas was agreed and is not to be changed for five years. No one could say what is expected for 1976.

The general principle in setting quotas is that each team should have enough to feed its members. Rich communes are selling a large proportion of their output and the poorest are selling little, or even receiving subsidies. This is the key to the apparent harmony of the Chinese economy compared to other developing countries, whether in the socialist or the market sphere. The surplus from agriculture, necessary for the growth of industry, is taken from those that find it least painful to part with and, indeed, from those who nowadays are eager to sell in order to have money to buy more from industry.

Teams who offer to sell more than their quota of grain receive a 30 per cent premium on the price. The fixing of the quota for five years means that most teams can look forward to increasing over-quota sales as productivity rises. In some cases they are advised to build up stocks instead of selling the extra grain or to use it to expand animal husbandry.

(Every household, team and commune is building up stocks of grain, and each commune has an emergency reserve, not to be used except in case of war or severe natural calamities.)

Cash crops, such as cotton, are sold on the basis of quotas but without a premium for above-quota sales. The trade in vegetables, fruit and meat with the commerce department is conducted in terms of contracts, not quotas. There is no problem of ensuring these supplies for the communes are eager to get contracts which provide an opportunity to earn money income all the year round.

The private markets are now quite a minor source of supply. Before the Great Leap they were said to provide 12 per cent of total retail sales; now the estimate is 2½ per cent.

Out-payments

The flow of money value of purchases from agriculture is balanced by a flow of purchases in the opposite direction. This counter flow of purchases by agriculture from industry comes partly from households and partly from brigades and communes.

As we have seen, there is a great circulation of money within a commune. Money comes into the teams for sales of grain, cash crops such as cotton and oil seeds, and for contract sales of vegetables. The team pays for fertiliser and for services such as tractor ploughing, grain milling and so forth. The former practice for the team as such to pay a contribution to the commune seems to be dying out as the commune's accumulation from its own factories and services increases; but the team, from time to time, may make a contribution to schemes of development which will increase its future production. The major part of the team's money income is distributed to households as payment for workpoints. The households pay a small fee for having their grain processed, for electric light, for building and so forth; part of their purchases from the retail shops are for local products such as fruit or sauces, while most are 'imported' from state or collective industry.

The brigades and the commune collect money from the services they provide to their members and from 'exports' from their industries. With this, they purchase fertilisers, electric power, agricultural machinery and equipment and materials for their industries.

Over and above the agricultural tax, agriculture contributes to the national revenue in respect to the element of tax and profit in the prices of the manufactured goods that are purchased by communes and by households. Prices of fertiliser and agricultural machinery are kept low as a matter of policy. Over the years since 1962, the terms of trade have shifted in favour of agriculture, as the prices of the main crops have been slightly raised and the prices of many manufacturers appreciably cut.

'The New Man'

The success of the Chinese economy in reducing the appeal of the money motive is connected with its success in economic development. When everyone has enough to eat today and hope of improvement tomorrow, when there is complete social security at the prevailing level of the standard of life and employment for all, then it is possible to appeal to the people to combat egoism and eschew privilege. It would not make much sense to the workers and peasants, say, in Mexico or Pakistan.

No doubt there are individuals in China with the temperamental itch for money, just as there are some people in the West who do not care about it. Individual temperaments are moulded by the setting in which they find themselves. The enormous pressure to commercialise every aspect of life in our society is substituted in China by an even stronger pressure the other way. 'Human nature' seems to fit it just as well, indeed, a good deal better, for the people whom one meets in China always seem much less nervous and ill-tempered than we are.

2. Political structure

To understand the process of economic planning, it is necessary to visiualise the structure of administration through which it operates.

The main political unit of the Republic are the provinces, inherited from imperial China. Besides, there are three autonomous cities (Peking, Shanghai and Tientsin), each with its surrounding rural area, and there are the autonomous regions inhabited by national minorities, having the same status as provinces. 'Province' is the usual translation of *sheng*.

Under the provinces are administrative districts roughly corresponding to the old prefectures — *zhuan* qü — and large cities. Under the districts, the rural areas are divided into counties — *xian* — and under the counties are smaller towns and communes. The communes are divided into brigades and teams. The cities are divided into urban districts — qü — and the districts are divided into neighbourhoods — *jiedao* — at roughly the same level as brigades, though of course their functions are quite different. Under the neighbourhoods are street committees, corresponding to teams. Large factories are independent units under the leadership of the provinces, smaller ones under districts or counties, and there are small collectives under the neighbourhoods. The phrase 'under the leadership' is always used in place of 'under control'.

The revolutionary committees, composed of cadres,* representatives of the enterprise's masses and members of the People's Liberation Army (or local militia), which emerged from the Cultural Revolution, have been regularised. There is now a revolutionary committee set up and run at every level from the provinces to the neighbourhood, the brigade and the enterprise. Each revolutionary committee has a standing committee which provides the executive, and at the higher levels, each has a staff of officials corresponding to a civil service.

At the centre, the old ministries still exist. The State Council, of which Chou En-lai is Premier, is composed of the Ministers.

The revolutionary committee, at each level, is described as the 'organ of political power'. This is a new conception of democracy which has no analogy with any other political system. A committee is composed of indi-

---

* The expression cadre (framework) in Western usage means the whole personnel of an administrative structure, for instance the corps of professional officers in an army. In the Soviet sphere, the word has come to be used for an individual. The Chinese expression *ganbu* was introduced as a translation of the Soviet sense of cadre; the root *gan* means 'to do' and *bu* part, section or ministry. The old term for 'officials' is not used because of its bad historical associations. The cadres, mostly, but not all, Party members, are those who have positions of special responsibility, at all levels.

viduals who have their own work to do in various spheres. Administration is carried out by a standing committee, corresponding, for instance, to the government of a province or the local authority of a county.

Parallel, at each level, are the Party committees, representing the Party members in each organisation. The Party, under the Central Committee, of which Mao Tse-tung is Chairman, is concerned with policy and political education and the revolutionary committees are charged with carrying out the Party's policy. There is usually a considerable overlap of membership between Party committees and the standing committees at each level, so that the executive organs are concerned in discussing policy. The main lines of policy must be determined in the Central Committee and carried down to the executive levels through the Party committees, but following Chairman Mao's conception: from the masses to the masses, the Party, at every level, is concerned also to convey feelings, ideas and suggestions up to the centre. The Party might be compared with the nervous system which conveys information to the brain as well as transmitting directions from the brain to the muscles.

I was given some details of the revolutionary committee of Shanghai, which ranks as a province. Others are on the same pattern. There are 150 members, of whom representatives of the masses are 105, cadres 21, and PLA representatives 24. The representatives of the masses consist of 43 workers, 21 peasants (from the counties surrounding the city), 8 Red Guards (now at middle school, no longer university students), 16 intellectuals, concerned with the arts and cultural activities, and 17 commercial workers.

The representation of the PLA on revolutionary committees is a legacy of the Cultural Revolution dating from the time before the Party was reconstituted. The PLA members are now concerned mainly with political education. At lower levels the representation seems to have become rather a formality.*

The committee as a whole meets generally twice a year, to hear a report on the year's work and to discuss the annual plan. It is responsible for appointing the standing committee which carries out the duties of the old provincial government. The administration of the province is carried out through bureaux concerned with planning, commerce, finance, education and health, and so forth, and there are corresponding departments at the lower levels.

An administrative district was formerly merely a subsidiary branch of the provincial administration, but now each has a revolutionary committee of its own and plays a considerable part in economic development. Many districts are in charge of factories and mines and, in some cases, take a share in the distribution of their output.

The counties have very important functions in advising and serving the

---

* See page 46.

communes, in developing the five small industries, collecting the agricultural tax, adjudicating over remissions in case of natural calamities and supervising the free markets.

The police and law courts are at the county and urban district level. There are no police in the communes.

The provision of education and the health service is primarily the responsibility of the provincial administration, but factories, neighbourhoods and brigades provide clinics and elementary schools. Many communes have small hospitals and middle schools. I came across a large enterprise some way outside a city that provided a hospital and schools for the families of its own workers and the neighbourhood. It included the salaries of doctors, teachers and nurses in its wage fund, so that they were reckoned as part of the cost of production of its output. The general principle seems to be that there should be enough hospitals and schools to meet requirements and that if one authority does not provide them another will.

Since the reconstitution of the Party and the restoration of 'one headquarters' after the turmoil of the Cultural Revolution, what power, in practice, is in the hands of the people? The 'basic units of political power' are the revolutionary committees of enterprises and neighbourhoods in the cities and brigades or communes in the country. It is clear enough that organised workers and peasants, especially after the Cultural Revolution, have a great deal of power over their own conditions of life — they can be led but not pushed. How about the neighbourhoods?

No one can be represented by two revolutionary committees at a similar level. The workers living in a particular neighbourhood, although participating in the local social and political activities, would be represented by the revolutionary committee in their factory. The neighbourhood represents mainly housewives and retired people. Street committees elect representatives and these are represented on the neighbourhood committee along with cadres and the PLA (though the PLA representation seems to be vestigial). The cadres at the neighbourhood level are paid salaries by the city. It is their business not only to bring down suggestions from above but also to carry the views of the people up. For instance, they collect the customers' views about the quality and variety of goods to the local shops. When some special task comes up, say a campaign to improve sanitation before the hot weather begins, meetings and discussions are held. The meetings may divide into groups under street committes. Plans can be modified according to the views that get support.

As a last resort, in case of grievances, there is still the good old method of writing big-character posters.* I asked, at a suburb of Shanghai, what was the last case when a poster was put up. I was told that, quite recently, a patient at the local hospital put up a complaint that some of the cadres

---

* People or groups write their views, suggestions and criticisms in big-characters on large sheets of paper and put them up in conspicuous places to be read and possibly refuted or challenged by others. They were first used in 1957. See page 44 for examples of recent posters.

there did not show concern for the people. On seeing the poster, the cadres called a meeting and investigated the matter. It turned out that a worker who was sick applied to a cadre to give him an authorisation to take leave from work but was brushed aside. Other cadres at the meeting realised that they too had been negligent; they accepted the criticism and resolved in future to take more care to keep in touch with the people.

So the right to criticise the Party, the heritage of the Cultural Revolution, is still kept alive down at the grass roots as well as in the important organisations of administration and production.

3. Planning

There are several phrases always used in connection with the system of economic planning — 'Two initiatives, of the top and of the bottom'; 'From the bottom up and from the top down'; and 'Leaving leeway', which means allowing room for adjustments as production goes on.

Proposals and demands from each level pass up to the province. Once a year, the representatives of all the provinces meet with the Planning Commission in Peking. Balances for production and distribution of all the main commodities, and for flows of finance, are made and agreed. Each province comes back with commitments and guarantees, which are then distributed down from level to level as firm undertakings.

The bureaucracy

There are various departments concerned in drawing up a provincial plan. The plan for agriculture gives targets for the major crops and for fisheries and forestry. It is also concerned with promoting mechanisation.

The plan for industry gives all major products in quantities and minor ones as a global sum. It makes allowance for trial production of new items.

There is a plan for communications and transport within the provincial orbit. The plan for commerce covers the volume of purchases of consumer goods to be supplied through the shops and matches the value of sales against total purchasing power.

The plan for capital construction sets out all major projects and the additional productive capacity that they will provide.

There is a plan for the labour force and the wage bill, showing the number of new jobs that will be created.

There are departments concerned with education, culture and health, dealing with enrolment in schools and colleges and with the medical service, sanitation and the arts.

The plan covers the distribution of materials and of the products of agriculture and industry.

Finally, there is a department concerned with finance, dealing with revenue and expenditure and setting targets for reduction of costs of production.

The revolutionary committee of a province is served by various bureaux concerned with these aspects of the plan, with appropriate staff. A similar apparatus of smaller dimensions is repeated at the district and county level.

Cadres at the commune and neighbourhood level are also on the pay roll of the province.

This bureaucracy is performing the functions, not only of the civil service in the capitalist countries, but also of a large part of private business. A socialist enterprise does not have a board of directors, a sales department or an account with an advertising agent. It has no concern with the Stock Exchange; its system of finance is very simple and it has no need for legal advice on tax dodging.

There is a continual campaign to prevent bureaucrats from behaving bureaucratically. A new kind of triple union has come into fashion — of the old, the middle-aged and young — combining experience, stamina and fresh ideas.

The keynote in planning is 'to grasp the policy of the Party and to mobilise the masses'. The bureaucracy was accused, during the Cultural Revolution, of dictating to the people instead of consulting them. They worked out plans in their offices, they thought that all that was needed could be done with three instruments, the computer, the telephone and the typewriter. They dealt in statistics, not reality; they thought in terms of materials and forgot about people.

The new style of planning is much more effective, for targets that have been accepted by the workers who will carry them out can be relied upon. When workers and management understand what they are supposed to be doing, they can discuss the difficulties that they meet within the course of production and resolve them. They understand how to analyse contradictions and so overcome them. A plan made in consultation with those who undertake to carry it out can set higher targets than bureaucratic methods would ever permit, with much greater assurance that they will be achieved.

The process of consultation goes down to the lowest level of political power all over the country.

Agriculture

In the communes in August and September, after the harvest, each team is called upon to review last year's work and to outline proposals for next year's production. No plan, of course, ever starts on a blank sheet; usually proposals are for the same as last year and as much more as possible. However, there may have been some important change in productive capacity, say, control of water has spread over a new area, or there may have been some change in policy from above, say, a request for more sugar or more cotton. In the light of all the conditions, the teams produce a statement of proposed output and of how much to consume for their own needs. Specialist teams put in their requirements of grain to purchase. (There are no direct deals between teams, brigades or communes except for such things as swaps of seed. Any transactions involving cash have to go up and down through a higher authority.) The proposals of teams are discussed with the commune and passed up to the county. The principle of leaving leeway means that plans are not too tight; there should be room for over-fulfilment, with a bit of effort. A higher authority will sometimes suggest a reduction rather than an increase in proposed output.

The county, after discussion with the communes, passes up the totals for each crop, through the district to the province.

Contracts for the supply of vegetables, eggs, fruit and meat to the cities are outside the plan and so are sales through the free market. The industrial investment of the communes and brigades, and the five small industries at county and district level are outside the plan, for these go down to foster agricultural development, not up to supply the industrial market. They may, however, involve requests, say, for a purchase of tractors, which must go into the province's demands on the central Planning Commission.

All main crops, grain, vegetables, edible oils, sugar, tobacco and cotton are dealt with under the national plan. The National Programme for Agricultural Development set targets for the per hectare yield of grains for the three main areas: North of the Yellow River, Chinling Range, Pailung River and areas north of the Yellow River in Chinghai Province — three tons per hectare; South of the Yellow River and North of the Huai River — 3.75 tons per hectare; South of the Huai River, and the Yangtse River — six tons per hectare. A northern commune that has topped the score of six tons claims to have 'crossed the Yangtse'.

For ginned cotton the targets are 300, 450, 600 and 750 kilogrammes per hectare for the different regions.

Each province is given an allocation for its own consumption. Surpluses from some are allocated to those which have deficits. In principle, a particular province has no more claim on the production within its own territory than has any other. At the annual meeting, each province must 'combat egoism' and take the needs of others into account. At the same time deficit provinces are strongly urged to increase production. (The area north of the Yellow River, formerly dependent on imports from the south, now claims to be producing as much grain as it consumes.)* Exports, foreign loans and gifts of agricultural products are provided for out of the surplus of production over the total planned consumption of the country as a whole.

After the meeting, the province's plan comes down again from level to level; at each level demands and allocations are shared out to the level below. There is a second round of meetings to discuss how each brigade and team is to produce its allotted share.

As the year goes by, successes are balanced against failures at each level, commune, district and county. The leeway in one plan can be used to offset a deficit in the fulfilment of another. Apart from very severe natural calamities, the province as a whole is expected to fulfil its plan. The surplus

* At the end of 1973 it was announced that several previously grain-deficient provinces could now produce as much as they consumed: Hopei, Shangtung, Honan, Northern Kiangsu and Anhwei.

it has agreed to hand over is the first priority; a short-fall has to be met by economising on consumption. Excess production may be utilised within the province, added to stock or put at the disposal of the centre.

Lines and areas: centralisation versus regional planning

The national government is directly responsible for the armed forces, central administration, main-line transport and foreign trade. In respect to industry, there has been an important change. Formerly all the large manufacturing enterprises were directly controlled by ministries at the centre. The enterprise received its plan of production and its allocation of materials from the ministry concerned. At an early stage, this may have been necessary, but as the industrial enterprise gained experience, it became a great nuisance. The familiar tales about over-centralisation in the Soviet Union are repeated about the old system. An enterprise wanting an extra hundred tons of cement, that could be supplied by the next county, had to write to Peking and wait months for permission to get it. In two adjacent provinces, an enterprise in one was given a plan for producing the mechanism of watches and in the other, the supply of cases, so that if either over-fulfilled its plan the other held it up. One enterprise was given small-sized ball bearings to produce, and another large ones, so that a machine-maker had to apply for supplies from both. Presumably under the excuse of economies of specialisation, this was a method of keeping power in the hands of the ministries, for no good purpose.

This is now called the 'dictatorship of the line'. Under the new system, production plans are made in terms of areas. Each of the enterprises formerly under central control has been given to the province where it is situated. Their output and requirements are now included in the local and provincial plan, so that neighbouring enterprises can concert their programmes and help each other out. Some specialisation is necessary but wherever possible all components are produced within a locality, partly for convenience and partly to promote self-sufficiency in case of war. Above-plan production is put at the disposal of the province or the city where an enterprise is situated.

Similarly, some enterprises formerly in the province's sphere have been put under district or county planning, and these are allowed to hand over a proportion of their output for local use.

When a new installation is to be set up, the locality organises a 'war of annihilation'. Neighbouring enterprises send some of their workers, and everyone, from the army to the Red Guards in the local schools, rallies round. By this means, a blast furnace at the Wuhan iron and steel complex was put up in four and a half months, and a larger one at Anshan in ten months.

The line, that is the branch of industry in the country as a whole, still has an important part to play in the planning system. An enterprise, like a commune, begins in the fourth quarter of the year to review its work and make proposals for next year. It is in touch with the appropriate ministry and with the provincial planners, so that it has a general idea of what its aim should be. The year's plan is discussed with representatives of the workers in each shop and a draft plan put to the province. The province carries the proposals of all its enterprises to the Planning Commission. Important commodities are given in quantities and the rest as a sum of money. The province brings back an agreed plan and parcels it out. When the targets and requirements of an enterprise have been settled at the area level, it is called to a meeting of the line, that is, the industry — iron and steel, machine tools, electrical equipment, textiles, or any one of several hundred branches. Representatives of enterprises in one line, from all over the country, come to the meeting and work out how to dovetail their plans with each other. They then enter into contracts stipulating quantities, quality and delivery dates of each product. The enterprises concerned with investment goods enter into contracts with other enterprises, both for supplies and deliveries; in the consumption-goods sector, final deliveries are arranged with the commerce department of the regions to which supplies are directed.

The national meeting is held at the end of December or beginning of January, but the final details may not come down to the enterprises for two or three months. They therefore make provisional contracts at the beginning of the year and carry on with production. In the middle of the year there is another round, at which firm contracts are made in accordance with the plan.

There are price lists for all standard products. For a new item, the producer proposes a price, based on costs, and negotiates with the buyer.

An enterprise which is exceeding its planned output over the year requires further supplies of raw materials. This is dealt with in three ways. The enterprise may apply to thc appropriate bureau of the provincial government for an addition to its plan. In this case the bureau is responsible for providing the necessary supplies. Or the enterprise may be able to organise some supplies locally or it may carry on with economy of materials or using substitutes. Major enterprises hold stocks of materials for two or three months' work so as to provide themselves with room to manoeuvre. The bureau arranges for the disposal of the extra output, which may be required to meet a deficiency elsewhere. Meetings are held between enterprises to work out arrangements.

There is evidently a certain element of hit or miss in this style of planning. At the present time, capacity to produce iron and steel is ahead of the flow of ore from the mines. 'Our blast furnaces are often hungry'. This is often attributed, like many other evils, to the policy of Liu Shao-chi, but obviously investment and technical progress have more scope in fabricating than in mining. A campaign to increase mining is now under way. Whatever may be the defects of this loose-jointed style of planning, it is certainly found to be a great improvement on the tight planning which China at first imitated from the Soviet Union.

The national plan, as well as the main crops, covers production and distribution of all other raw materials and all the main items of industrial equipment; it covers also a large range of consumption goods such as textiles — yarn, piece-goods and knitwear — rubber boots, thermos flasks, bicycles, sewing machines. Other industrial products such as towels, china, leather shoes, are controlled by the provinces, and minor items such as small tools, buttons and baskets, are at the local level. At one time matches were included in the national plan, now they are supplied locally. Vehicles and tractors are under the national plan; other farm machinery is at the provincial or county level. All commodities under the national plan are distributed nationally. A contract to purchase can be made only in accordance with an allocation that has been granted. Under the plan, as with grain, no province has a prescriptive right to goods produced within it, but this rule is evidently not pushed too hard. Shanghai, which is the main industrial centre, keeps enough of its own production to make its department stores the envy of Asia.

Prices

All those commodities that come into the national plan have nationally fixed prices. Those controlled by the provinces have prices fixed in agreement with each other, so that there will not be different price levels on two sides of a boundary. Prices for small collectives are agreed with the factories to which they sell.

When the purchase price of grain was raised, to encourage production during the bad years, the retail selling price was kept unchanged. This avoided the vicious circle of inflation which is inevitable when food prices rise, so that urban wages have to be raised, which raises money demand for food and so on round. Till today, grain is sold in town at prices that do not cover the full cost of transport and handling. (In Shanghai the subsidy is said to be about 10 per cent of total sales value.)

The whole industrial price level is built up on the price of grain, for this determines the cost of living, and so the lowest wage rate. Higher grades of wages are erected on that base, which thus determines the whole wage and salary bill for industry, commerce and administration.

The cost of production of each commodity is made up of cost of materials (which depends on costs at an earlier stage or on purchase prices in agriculture), cost of power, the wage and salary bill, and depreciation. An allowance for depreciation of buildings and plant is at a flat rate of so much per year of its estimated life time. The costs of particular items of production are calculated individually; I did not try to find out how overheads and depreciation are allocated between items — a tiresome question which is not at all important, as evidently they are allocated somehow.

There is then a tax (except for goods which are to be sold at or below cost) and a planned profit, each expressed as a percentage of the value of output at ex-factory prices. The distinction between tax and profit seems to be administrative rather than economic. Together they make up what corresponds to the net profit margin in capitalist industry.

The tax rate most often quoted was 7 per cent of ex-factory prices. The profit for particular commodities is set according to their uses. For chemical fertiliser it is very low because this is an input for agriculture. For wine and cigarettes they are highest, though by no means high by our standards — 60 per cent of selling prices. Bicycles, watches, woollen cloth are high-priced items. (A bicycle costs three times the average monthly wage.)

Means of production are not exempted from contributing to the national revenue. Steel, as well as a tax of 7 per cent of ex-factory prices, carries a profit rate of 15 per cent. Machine tools carry 20 per cent. Small collectives producing components for equipment also pay 7 per cent tax and earn 20 per cent profit (of which they generally keep half for an accumulation fund).

According to the Soviet view, it is irrational to include profits in the prices of investment goods, since the state both gets the profit and pays for investment. However, the argument tells just as well the other way — since the state is going to get the profit back it does not matter that it pays it. Moreover, machinery is sold to the communes and other collectives, and some items, such as sewing machines, are sold both to industry and to households; the element of profit in these sales is contributing to national revenue. However that may be, the price system has evolved by a historical process, adjusted from time to time by common sense not by any doctrinal theory of value.

For goods controlled by the national plan, a standard is chosen of a good average production (not the very best) and the output of other enterprises is priced in relation to it. Thus, bicycles produced in Wuhan have a higher cost than in Shanghai, but they are considered to be not of such good quality; they are sold at a lower price and consequently carry a lower profit. The enterprise is called upon to increase efficiency and catch up with Shanghai. A low-cost chemical fertiliser plant has to carry a profit of 10 per cent, to even up its price with others which have higher costs and carry only 5 per cent. Over and above ex-factory prices, there is a general business tax of 3 per cent on turnover paid by the commerce department. There is a wholesale margin varying around 10 per cent for different commodities and a retail margin around 12 per cent. Services such as hotels, laundries, buses, etc. pay a tax on the basis of receipts at rates from 3 to 15 per cent.

The economic principle of planning retail prices is to ensure an overall value of sales that will absorb the overall flow of purchasing power coming from the total money income of the community. The money income of the community consists of the wage and salary bill, including welfare funds and proceeds of sales from communes, that enter into the costs of goods to be sold. Expenditure from the incomes earned in producing them covers this part of their costs. There are also incomes earned in administration, the armed forces, investment and social services. The expenditure from these incomes is absorbed by the surplus (profit and tax) in the sales value of goods sold to the public and this must also cover the element of subsidy in the sales of other commodities.

When prices are set too low, there is excessive demand and the temptation to create a black market. When prices are set too high, purchasing power is deficient and goods remain unsold. When the overall price level is correctly set, the surplus, that is the excess of the sales value of consumption goods over their own costs, matches the excess of total income over these costs, so that there is neither excess nor deficiency of demand relatively to supply. The Chinese authorities have been remarkably successful in maintaining this balance through good times and bad.

Subject to overall balance, social policy requires that the pattern of prices is such as to catch purchasing power from relative luxuries, while making it possible for the lowest income to afford the necessaries of life. In this respect, also, Chinese policy seems to succeed pretty well.

Besides keeping down the cost of living, subsidies are used to steer demand in particular directions; for instance, a kind of detergent, a by-product of a petro-chemical process, is sold very much below cost, while soap made from soya-bean oil — a precious material — is priced high.

So far, production has kept a step ahead of the growth of population; average consumption, by all accounts, seems to have been rising markedly in the last three years.

Investment

In the countryside, a great deal of investment is organised by communes, using labour in the slack season to carry out works of land reclamation and water control. Districts and counties also organise such schemes. Minor ones they merely report, but major ones, say a reservoir of more than 100 million cubic metres of capacity, have to be sanctioned in the national plan.

For industry, the investment plan 'takes the whole country as the chess board'. All major construction of new installations or enlargements of existing ones is allotted to particular places. The Five Year Plan lays out a general scheme of development and this is implemented year by year. At the annual national meeting, every province has put in schemes of investment and the centre has to ration them out. Major schemes are conceived in terms of the line — the need to increase productive capacity of particular types, and carried out in terms of areas — put into the plan of a particular province to be developed at a particular site.

The system of working through the administrative levels evidently facilitates geographical planning — each county knows the physical and the human possibilities of its own area. The district has to judge between the claims of counties and the province between the claims of districts. The general trend of policy at the top is to develop the hinterland and as far as possible to build up the whole range of industry in every region. The old centres are called upon to set up and man entire enterprises in far away places.

To economise investible resources, established enterprises must aim to increase productivity. The Anshan iron and steel complex is proud of increasing output between 1970 and 1971 by 10 per cent without requiring any additional equipment or manpower. (This was mentioned as an example of the superiority of the area over the line in the organisation of production.) In Shanghai, a small iron foundry, employing 200 workers and staff, offered to raise its planned output from 3,100 tons to 3,500. The city asked them if they could not do better. They thought it over and found that they were working 'four days hot and three days cold'; to give the workers one day off in seven, they let the furnace out the day before and took a day to get it going again afterwards. They arranged to stagger off-days, and so kept the furnaces going continuously. Their planned output for 1972 is 5,000 tons. A capitalist employer, of course, would insist on efficiency, but then he might have a strike on his hands. 'Raising the political consciousness of the workers' is much more economical.

Every enterprise, even in light industry, has a machine shop and is continually improving its equipment and gradually mechanising labour-intensive processes for itself.

In some provinces, enterprises at the district level are allowed to keep part of their profits for accumulation. Collectives at the county or neighbourhood level generally keep half their profits. The large enterprises are free to use their amortisation allowances to expand capacity.

Thus, in industry as well as in the communes there is a large amount of investment, in small packets all round the country, over and above the large schemes promoted in the national plan.

There is still a great deal of transport by mule or by human being — the stock of trucks is slowly increasing and motor boats (of cement instead of timber) are gradually displacing oars and sails on the river.

'Self-reliance and hard work' is the watchword now. It is gradually nibbling away at the huge mass of accumulation that is needed to make work a little less hard for everyone.

Anti-pollution

The authority of the area over the line is a great help in the campaign against pollution. The authorities of an area are concerned with the health of their inhabitants and the amentities of town and countryside, while the line is more apt to emphasise production for its own sake. It is natural enough for the management of a heavy-industry enterprise to be rather bored by complaints that require it to deflect its energies from what it sees as its proper purpose.

The negative concept of pollution is unwelcome in China. The problem is phrased in a positive way as a campaign to eliminate the three wastes, of gas, water and materials, and to turn them to good use. Valuable minerals are extracted from smoke. 'This, which was formerly poison, is now a treasure'. Channels are built to carry water, purified, for irrigation and the contamination extracted from it is turned into fertiliser. Old vehicles and machinery are carried off to commune workshops and turned into spare parts. Scraps of leather are turned into shoddy good enough for making camera cases.

There is a lot that still needs to be done. Not so long ago, a plume of black smoke curling into the air beside an ancient pagoda was a scene for pride and joy. It goes against the grain rather to have to view it as a menace. But while capitalist cities smother themselves in smog, blue skies will become a still greater source of pride before long.

Employment

In China there is no problem of unemployment. Each commune finds jobs for its children as they grow up and a proportion of school-leavers from the cities are sent into the country. Any labour not required for cultivation is put on to construction or production in small factories, at first 'with bare hands' and then gradually mechanised.

Each industrial enterprise has its complement of workers, technicians and cadres. Wastage is made good by applying to the provincial or municipal labour bureau for replacements, but any increase in numbers has to be sanctioned by the Planning Commission. The same applies to commerce, administration and social services. When an increase in personnel is permitted, the enterprise or office is instructed where to go for recruits. Many will be young people originally from the city who have served their two years on a commune; others are drawn from the peasantry. There is an unlimited pool of labour in the countryside to supply industry and plenty of young people who are eager to come. (Indeed, in spite of all efforts at regulation, it is not possible altogether to eliminate infiltration into towns. Shanghai, in particular, is an irresistible attraction.)

The counties can recruit for their small industries outside the national plan provided that they do not take more than 5 per cent of the agricultural labour force.

Housewives in cities are encouraged to work in small collectives or in the neighbourhood services that support them.

Activity in an industrial enterprise depends on the flow of materials. When there is a hold-up, the management will scrounge around and see if supplies are available anywhere. If not, the workers can be put on to improving equipment or cleaning the place up. At worst, they have more time for study. (In May 1972, everyone in China was reading a translation of extracts from Engels' *Anti-Dühring* — some elderly housewives were finding it difficult.)

Population

There is a strong propaganda campaign for late marriage and small families. Every kind of birth control facility is available either free or at low prices in town and country. The official aim is to get the rate of growth of population down to 1 per cent per annum.

In the cities, it seems, that the two-child family is in fashion, but in the countryside birth control is not enough to ensure a low birth rate. Peasants, even when they have become commune members, positively like having babies and, when they are enjoying prosperity hitherto unknown, they find it hard to see why they should not have families of three or four at least. However, the recent announcement that population (including Taiwan) has not yet reached 800 million shows that the campaign is more successful than foreign observers expected. The Chinese have stated that while the average annual rise in population since 1949 has been two per cent, the average increase in grain output for the same period was four per cent.

The question is often raised, how many bodies the territory of China can feed and clothe. (Clothing is a serious burden, for some hangover of Confucian notions of decency makes people cover themselves all day from wrist to ankle, even in the torrid south.) The existing cultivable area is very densely populated, but there is a great deal of empty space that could be broken in. However, the upper limit to the population is really beside the point. The important consideration is that any growth of numbers retards development. There is a limit to the proportion of activity that can be devoted to investment at any moment, and a given rate of investment can raise the average per head of equipment in agriculture and industry, and of housing and other amenities, faster the smaller the growth of numbers requiring to be brought up to the existing average. It is true that with every mouth God sends a pair of hands, but he does not send a tractor, a power station or even a schoolroom.

Chinese spokesmen are shy of discussing the growth of population as a menace but policy seems to indicate that the leadership has grasped the point, though their policies cannot act fast.

Meanwhile, everyone who does get born is guaranteed work to do, an income and a place in society.

Finance

Along with the national plan expressed in physical terms, there is a plan in terms of finance.

About 20 per cent of national revenue comes from central sources, transport, foreign trade and customs. The rest comes from payments from those provinces which have an excess of revenue over expenditure. The expenditure from the central budget, besides the cost of defence, administration, higher education and foreign aid, consists of subventions to deficit areas — particularly the autonomous regions — and the finance of major investment projects.

The aim of financial policy is to ensure that the central budget balances, with a small surplus; this keeps the whole national income in balance. Revenue grows from year to year with the growth of the value of output, but it does not grow smoothly. With the spread of water control, violent fluctuations in agricultural output have been eliminated, but crops still vary from year to year. The value of production in terms of money depends upon the prices set on the various elements in total output. The pattern of prices is such that agriculture is reckoned to contribute only 20 per cent of national income, but it is still the key to growth. When the harvest has been good and the revenue correspondingly buoyant, more schemes of investment can be started in next year's plan, and when the growth has been small, new plans for next year will be restrained.

The secret of carrying out development without inflation is to keep the flow of output of consumption goods in step with the growth of the money-wage bill. By tailoring the growth of investment to the growth of the agricultural surplus and by keeping a judicious mixture of quick-yielding investments in light industry with large long-term projects, the Chinese planners seem to have succeeded in maintaining 'balanced, proportional growth' up till now, through good times and bad.

For a province, under the system now in force, there is no conception of balancing the budget or of raising revenue to provide for expenditure. Each province has a planned revenue and a planned expenditure which have no connection with each other. Western readers have difficulty in grasping this principle. We think of the income of a unit as that which it has a right to dispose of. In the Chinese financial system this is not the case. The two sides of a provincial budget are quite separate. Its revenue is its contribution to national funds and its expenditure is the share of national funds allotted to it.

Shanghai, the richest unit, has planned expenditure, including centrally financed investment within its boundaries, of 10 per cent of its revenue. A province in the old industrial North East has expenditure of 18 per cent of revenue, excluding central investment; a province in the central region, 30 per cent, and so on. The autonomous regions have planned revenue which is much less than expenditure. For example, since 1960 the bulk of Tibet's budget has been financed and 30 per cent of its grain supply provided by the central authorities. By this means, the government is taxing the relatively richer part of the population to cover its own outlay and to even up development for the poorest.

The revenue of a province comes from the agricultural tax, the taxes and profits of state enterprises in industry, commerce and services, and taxes, and about half the profits from collective factories. There are some minor items, such as bicycle licences.

Planned expenditure, apart from investment, consists of salaries and miscellaneous expenses for administration (down to the level of communes and neighbourhoods), education, the health service and some urban housing (much of housing is provided by enterprises for the workers and counts as part of their initial investment).

The province is also allowed some contingency funds for extra expenditure in case of need. Any saving which a province makes out of its planned expenditure, it is allowed to keep. Formerly an excess over planned revenue was passed to the central budget; after the Cultural Revolution, to encourage initiative, the province was allowed to keep it, but for 1972 it has been decided to set a ceiling to the excess revenue, above which any further excess is divided half and half with the centre.

The province allocates planned revenue and planned expenditure to districts and counties, and applies the same or similar rules to them.

The financial relations of the centre with the provinces are regulated by 'three uniformities and three privileges'.

The uniformities are first, the rule that national financial policy is determined at the centre; second, allocations of investment and expenditure are made under the central budget; no change can be made without approval from Peking. And the financial system is uniform over the whole country — tax rates, wage and salary rates and the prices of the main products are determined centrally.

The privileges are first, the right to make adjustments between localities and enterprises. Once the total of revenue and expenditure have been set, the province can allocate them as it finds convenient. Secondly, the province is free to dispose of the surplus arising from under-planned expenditure and over-planned revenue (subject to the rule concerning a ceiling) and its contingency allowances, with the restriction that it may not use these funds to increase personnel employed or to raise wages. Thirdly, the province has the right to implement the plan that has been given to it in its own way, subject to the principles of government policy.

The provinces and under them districts, counties, neighbourhoods, communes, state enterprises and collectives are all expected to preserve strict financial discipline, though no individual or corporate income is in any way dependent on it. The secret of operating such a system evidently lies in the extremely high standard of civic morality that everyone expects of everyone else, and in its openness. Everyone has to live up, not only to the demands of his superiors but also to the standards that the masses below require of him.

4. Struggle, criticism, transformation

'You ask about the Cultural Revolution. I'll tell you my own experiences'. The chairman of the revolutionary committee, that is the director, of a textile factory in Peking, is speaking to the foreign visitors. 'I was deputy director at that time, a Party member since 1956. When it all began in 1966, I did not understand what was going on. I didn't know how to take it. I could not grasp the issues. Two lines, two headquarters, it did not make sense. When I was criticised by the workers, I was aggrieved. Didn't I work hard, come early and leave late, carry out all my duties conscientiously? The more they attacked me, the less I understood. I became quite bewildered and could not carry on. The workers cried: Stand aside. They made me go to work on the shop floor. I was working as a machine-minder from January to November 1967. I thought to myself: Let's see how you manage the factory. I felt it was just as well to be working on the shop floor, for I knew that I might have made mistakes and as long as I was in a prominent position I should be fired at. The workers criticised my methods of management; they said I was a boss. They linked me with Liu Shao-chi. I could not understand it but I lost my self-confidence. What was it all about? Hadn't I been a good party member? I was quite confused.

'There were two factions among the workers: *East is Red* and *Red Rebels*. A work team had been sent (as I realise now) by the Liu party and had set up a so-called Cultural Revolution committee. The factions formed in disputing about it, but they very soon forgot all about criticising revisionism; they were only interested in criticising each other. When it came to discussing the cadres in the factory, the *East is Red* group thought that I might still be useful, but the *Red Rebels* were "down-with-everything" boys. They were against all cadres. "Suspect all, depose all" was their watchword. I tagged along with *East is Red*. I just had to do as they did and keep quiet.

'I am glad to say that it did not come to blows with us as it did in many places, but the situation was really absurd. Both groups were working, but they would not speak to each other; one would not pass a tool to another. Each lot said to the others: We can carry on production without your help. There were two factions in every workshop. All the cadres were doing manual work, and the workers were carrying on as they pleased. All rules and regulations were defied. There were rival loud speakers set up on the premises, blaring away at each other all the time. Some output was produced but of course it fell far below normal.

'Then in June 1967, a group of Liberation Army men came in. They were really amazing; they were so calm and patient. They did not begin by shouting at anybody but settled down to study and investigate to find out what had caused the trouble. They came to the conclusion that both factions were good revolutionaries but that both had some faults. They set about to get them together. It was hard work. Neither gang would admit that the others were any good. The army men had the greatest difficulty in persuading them to sit on the same bench.

'On September 14, 1967, came the Chairman's new instructions, saying that there was no fundamental cause for conflict within the working class. The PLA men had it printed and distributed copies not only in the workshops but to the workers' homes as well. They kept on talking to the workers, in groups and one by one. Sometimes they would have 12 or 15 interviews with one man.

'On September 19 the army men got the two factions to unite formally, but they were still not agreed ideologically. The army men held study courses on the theme of "combat egoism". They got each faction to make self-criticism. In November, the revolutionary committee was formed. There were wrangles till the last minute; it took three days to choose representatives. It was decided to have 15 members and one faction claimed the right to appoint 11. However, in the end it was settled at eight and seven. All the same, some ultra-left ideas remained. It took a long time to get things straight.

'As far as I was concerned personally, I know now that I had a lot of wrong ideas. The army men instituted study of the question of cadres early in August. They put us through it for two months. They made us study the Chairman's *Investigation of the Peasant Movement in Hunan*. I thought: Goodness, I read that years ago. I did not like the idea of having to criticise myself. I still thought I had always done a good job. Besides, this article was all about the wicked landlords. Am I a landlord? But the army men persisted and got us to read seriously. It took me two and a half weeks. Then one day we came on the passage: "In a very short time . . . several hundred million peasants will rise like a mighty storm. . . . There are three alternatives. To march at their head and lead them. To trail behind them, gesticulating and criticising. Or to stand in their way and oppose them". It suddenly struck me with terrific force. Yes, I had been dragging behind; I had been an obstacle to the revolution. "Without the poor peasants there would be no revolution. To deny their role is to deny the revolution. To attack them is to attack the revolution". Now it had a meaning for me. I saw everything in a new light. The workers had attacked me but the main point was to overthrow revisionism. What did personal gain or loss count beside that? The socialist state must not change its colour.

'I also re-read the three beloved articles. How did I compare with Norman Bethune? Was it right to be offended and to stop serving the people because I had been criticised? I had a struggle with myself and I admitted that I had made mistakes and I determined to correct them. I came to understand that I had ultra-left ideas myself. Then I had to go to the workers and find out what they thought of me. I took a portrait of the

Chairman in my hands and a quotation about combatting egoism, and presented myself to one group of workers after another. I felt foolish at first and I was frightened at what they would say. I thought they would never forgive me. But, to my delight, they welcomed me. They said: "It was a pity you did not start coming to us sooner". They said: "We only criticised you to make you one of the Left instead of the Right". They hoped I would not lose touch with them again. It took me three days to go round all the workshops. In the end I was elected on to the revolutionary committee and now I am chairman. Most of the high and middle cadres were also rehabilitated.

'But the problem of ultra-leftism was not completely solved. It came up during the process of purifying the class ranks and in the reorganisation of management.

'The main reason for the persistence of ultra-left ideas was that we had not studied well but there was also the influence of "May 16" agents. They opposed Chairman Mao's line, they were counter-revolutionary but they put on the cloak of the ultra-left. There were some sinister elements right at the top. Most of their followers were simply misled.

'From the winter of 1970 there was a campaign against the ultra-left. Their ideas were criticised and the "May 16" elements were exposed and repudiated. The principle was followed of educating the many and eliminating the few; of drawing lessons from past mistakes to avoid them in the future, and curing the disease to save the patient.

'As far as our factory is concerned, there were some workers who followed the ultra-left line, but they were influenced by leaders from outside. We organised a course of study and over a year most of those who had been misled saw that they had been wrong. There is only one man still left in the study course, and we do not believe that he is a real counter-revolutionary.

'After this the problem of ultra-left ideas was much less serious. Now we have established the socialist democratic style of management. Of course, it is not perfect. There is still work to be done.'

This conversation was the most vivid of several covering the same ground. There is no lack of references to 'the period of anarchy' and a senior man will recount to inquisitive foreigners how he was criticised by the workers and returned to his position only after recognising his mistakes.

In the Sixteen Points, which set out the scenario for the Cultural Revolution, it is stated that 95 per cent of cadres are 'good or partly good'. Whatever may have happened at the top, at lower levels of administration it seems that much less than five per cent have been finally got rid of.

It is to be observed that in the above story there is no distinction drawn between the Liu line and the ultra-left. One stood for deference, hierarchy and monetary incentives, the other for 'Down with everything', yet they are regarded as essentially the same because the consequences of both were equally counter-revolutionary.

The mysterious 'May 16' conspiracy is generally blamed for violent excesses and for fermenting factional strife. When Chou En-lai apologised, by implication, for the burning of the British Chancelry in Peking, saying it was the work of 'bad elements', he is taken to have been referring to the 'May 16' group. We all know that it does not need any conspiracy to make young people break the bands of discipline when they get a chance, or fall into quarrels over points of abstract principle. There is certainly evidence that there were sinister characters taking advantage of these natural impulses; but perhaps the sinister element is sometimes exaggerated in telling the story and natural impulse played down.

After the reconciliation of factions and the creation of revolutionary committees, came the process of 'cleaning the ranks', and the reconstitution of the Party. Then a thorough overhaul of the system of management was instituted in every enterprise. The Anshan Constitution, 'putting politics in command' was originally promulgated in 1960. It is now being given new life. During the upheaval of the cultural revolution, the workers had got rid of the 'kuang-kuang' — a picturesque phrase translated as 'irrational rules'. Formerly the rules were ridiculously detailed, down to a precise list of things that a toddler had to bring to nursery school. The book of regulations for a factory employing five thousand workers and staff contained 320,000 characters, couched in a high-falutin' style that the workers could not follow. Management was unnecessarily compartmentalised. A worker's suggestion for a technical improvement had to pass through a dozen offices before it could be accepted. The system of making cadres work on the shop floor for a month every year was often reduced to a formality.

But in tearing up the 'kuang-kuang', the workers tore up too much. When they got production going again, they realised that 'because management must be simplified, it does not mean that there is no need for management; because cadres are sent to work at the bench, it does not mean that there is no need for cadres, and because irrational rules are abolished, it does not mean that there is no need for any rules.'

Now the process of reforming the system of management is still going on in many enterprises. All rules and regulations are discussed with the workers in each shop and introduced when they have proved acceptable. One-man management on the Soviet model has disappeared, but the leadership of the chairman of the revolutionary committee — that is the director of an enterprise — is indispensable. As one director said with a wry smile: 'The achievements of our enterprise are due to collective work, but if anything goes wrong, it is my responsibility.'

Sometimes during 'the period of anarchy' accounting was completely abolished — the workers maintained that provided they produced the stuff, what did the cost matter? However, when they looked into it, at a particular machine-tool plant, they found that hours of work for a certain item had not been checked and the enterprise to which it was sold had been over-charged by a total of 20,000 yuan. When the mistake was discovered, the excess was repaid.

The cadres who have been restored to authority are still subject to criticism from below; they must avoid putting on bossy airs. But there are some rules that have to be made obligatory. For instance, if a man is late for work, he is admonished; if he persists, he will be formally criticised; if he still does not mend his ways, he will have to be punished. What is the punishment? It will be placed on his record.

No one is ever sacked except for a serious crime. This is rare. In a complex with a personnel of 150,000, they had not had a case since the Cultural Revolution began.

5. Industrial management

The rules of management are laid down under seven heads:

1. There is a clear demarcation of responsibility. Each cadre and each worker knows his responsibilities.
2. Attendance is obligatory. A doctor's certificate is needed for sick leave. In case of family problems, the factory decides whether to grant leave. (For women workers, there is statutory leave of eight weeks for childbirth.)
3. Standard methods of technical operation are laid down for each process.
4. Standards of quality are laid down for each stage of production. The individual worker is responsible for observing them. There is a final inspection, but inspection cannot do everything; no defective goods should be allowed to leave the factory.
5. Each group is responsible for maintenance of its equipment. Machinery should be regularly checked. Minor repairs are carried out on the spot and there is a special workshop for major repairs.
6. Safety and the health of workers must be considered. This is the concern of the factory as a whole, the workshop and the working group. Ventilation, dust extraction, etc. should be installed. Protective clothing, boots and spectacles must be provided where necessary.
7. There must be strict accounting. The wage bill, cost of labour production, cost of materials and depreciation of equipment and buildings must be allocated among particular products.

These rules were drawn up much earlier but they have been reanimated by the transformation of management that follows from the Cultural Revolution. Now management has to co-operate with the workers in the application of rules, and workers co-operate with management.

In each work group, there is an elected representative responsible for a particular aspect of the conduct of the group. These representatives are concerned with such matters as planning — that is, discussing the group's contribution to the draft plan put up by the enterprise, the distribution of jobs under the final plan, and fulfilment of quotas of work; check on punctuality and attendance; safety regulations and care in observing them; (many factories have now adopted the system of bare-foot doctors from the communes and most have professional medical workers attached to the staff); technical operations; quality control; inventions and technical improvements; maintenance of equipment; provision for the livelihood of the workers — housing, the flow of supplies to the local shops and so forth;

entertainment, including amateur musical and theatrical groups; political study and discussion; and supervision of the use of materials and avoidance of waste. For a factory as a whole, representatives responsible for economy in production are invited to scrutinise important items of expenditure.

In some enterprises, only four or five of these topics are covered by special representatives in the work groups; health and welfare are never omitted.

The Party, at every level, is concerned with political study and discussion and with mobilising the masses to play their part in planning, management, technical progress and production.

There is a trade union organisation (*gong hui* — workers' organisation or association) based on the workshop and factory. These units elect representatives to the wider trade union organisations up to the municipal and provincial levels. A Peking factory of 1,300 workers, for instance, has a factory trade union committee of sixteen members (nine of whom are women).*

There are representatives of workers on the revolutionary committee and the Party committee of each enterprise. A member of the revolutionary committee is obliged to resign if workers raise objections to his conduct. This is rare, but not unknown.

Technicians and cadres are expected to spend at least a third of their time at the bench. Formerly they produced designs 'behind closed doors' and handed them down. Now all designs are discussed with the workers who will have to put them to use.

There are part-time schools at which workers are able to qualify themselves as technicians. Individuals may be moved round to get experience of different processes. (In one factory, the management insisted on workers taking a turn as helpers in the canteen kitchen, so as to raise the status of what was traditionally considered a menial job.)

In playing down monetary incentives, Chinese industry appeals to what are evidently much more effective motives.

---

* The functions of trade unions in China, where the workers see themselves as 'the masters of the factory not the slaves of production' are quite different from those of trade unions in the West.

During the Cultural Revolution the trade unions were found to be riddled with bad elements who negated the class struggle. In 1966, the trade unions were disbanded and in 1968, a provisional form of organisation, 'workers' representative congresses' (*gong-ren dai-biao da-hui*) were formed.

The New Year Message in 1973 called for the consolidation 'step by step' of the trade unions (*gong hui*) and other mass organisations. There followed in April 1973 congresses of trade unionists in Peking and Shanghai and in June, July and August in all of China's provinces.

Today, the functions of the trade unions are said to be mainly to organise study and raise political consciousness as well as to pay attention to the workers' welfare, and assist in the training of worker-cadres.

6. Neighbourhood factories

Some of the small collectives, mainly staffed by housewives, are working as subsidiaries of large factories. This is industry at the stage of the putting-out system. Highly labour-intensive processes, such as hand-sewing uppers of shoes or painting toys, are given to the collectives, where housewives work near home in rooms provided by the neighbourhood. Others have progressed to quite sophisticated products.

One housewives' collective in Peking that began by repairing scales now supplies highly specialised equipment for the electronics industry. They send a representative to the annual meeting of the line to discuss their part in the plan.

In 1958, during the Great Leap, six young people in Nanking got together to start glass-blowing in half a room. They produced test tubes. In 1960, when the Soviet contracts were broken, they were asked to produce mercury switches needed in power stations. One type, that had come from Czechoslovakia, required a tubular glass ring with a very fine wire running round inside it. They managed to make the ring by winding heat-softened glass round an iron bar, but how to get the wire in it? The could scarcely eat or sleep for a week while they racked their brains. One day a member of the group was going by bus to a meeting, thinking about their problem. Suddenly there came into his mind a folk--tale about an emperor who set a problem for his daughter's suitors. He had a wooden tube made with nine zigzag bends, and declared that whoever could pass a single thread of silk through it should have the princess. All the generals and mandarins failed, but the carpenter's son tied the thread to an ant which ran through the tube.

The young glass-blower passed his bus stop and forgot all about the meeting. He rushed back and told his mates the story. Some ran out to catch ants but one had a more feasible idea; he remembered that glass does not insulate from a magnet. They found that they could fasten a fragment of steel to the wire and lead it round the tube. They have been using this method ever since. They never found out how the Czechs did it.

The business now employs workers in several houses. Some of its products are exported. Its planning level has been elevated from the neighbourhood to the urban district.

Neighbourhood factories existed from early days, but the Cultural Revolution gave the movement a new impetus.

In Shengyang, after reading Chairman Mao's statement of 16 May 1966, nine housewives (the oldest was 56) decided that they must do something.

They learned from some old workers that pressings can be made from metal powder and that there is iron oxide in the waste thrown out from sintering works. They decided to master the process and start work. The neighbours were startled. Many supported them but some men jeered. 'Women are better at making noodles than metal powder' (a pun in Chinese). Undeterred, they found an empty site on waste land in their housing estate. They borrowed five spades from a nearby commune and two cauldrons from a chemical plant. At first they had to work in the open air, running for shelter when the rain was too heavy and going back when it lightened, stamping their feet and blowing on their fingers in the winter. They would not take a loan from the state; they were to do it all by their own efforts.

They collected broken fire bricks from a refectory plant to line their kiln and got building bricks of slag for their workshops. They welded old tar-drums to make a chimney stack. Their husbands helped them on Sundays.

At first all the work of washing and of sorting the iron from the waste by magnets was done by hand. They keep their first equipment as a little museum in their first shed — a revolutionary heirloom to keep in mind and to show new generations the spirit of 'self-reliance and hard struggle'.

They now have 167 workers, of whom 30 are men, and they have got together workable equipment, mainly fixed up by themselves. After the iron has been extracted and baked, it is first crushed in barrels turned on the principle of a spindle, as the old women suggested, and ground on the principle of a mangle. They produce gear casings and other components for which they contract with a number of factories. Prices are set to cover cost, tax of 5 per cent and profit of 20 per cent, of which they keep 45 per cent for accumulation.

It was typical of modern China that after one of the original nine had given the foreign visitors a vivid account of all stages of their technical development, it was necessary to send for the accountant to answer questions about prices and profits.

The neighbourhood provides a creche and nursery school for a small fee. The welfare fund pays wages during maternity leave and a subscription to the neighbourhood clinic.

The factory works on two shifts. Husbands have an agreement that whoever gets home first will cook the meals.

7. Self reliance

When the Soviet technicians were withdrawn in 1960, taking their blueprints with them, it was a severe shock to the Chinese economy, but a few years later it was being described as a bad thing turned into a good thing. One way or another, Chinese technicians solved the problems that the Russians left behind. Solutions adapted to their own conditions and requirements were far more effective than any they could take over from foreign experts.

Stories like that of the mercury switches are often repeated, though due acknowledgement is always made of help from Soviet technicians in early days.

Another tale comes from a big fertiliser plant which decided that it should make nylon filaments from a by-product of the main process. Their Soviet adviser told them that it was a highly sophisticated technique. They had better export soya beans to pay for nylon. However, they persisted and had placed an order for two pumps of the special type required.

When the technicians were withdrawn and the pumps refused, they determined to find out the secret and make the pumps themselves. After many experiments, they succeeded and set the process going.

Five years later, the Soviet Ambassador heard of it and wanted to see what was going on. He was invited to a visit and to lunch at the works. During the morning tour, they showed him the pumps at work and said: 'We are most grateful to you, for without your intervention we should never have made these pumps'. He left before lunch.

These tales are told with humour and with glee. They speak of a deep satisfaction that sweetens toil and sublimates personal ambition. Chinese patriotism and socialist ideology are pulling together, and every individual can see in his own little corner what that can achieve.

In this atmosphere, even the dreariest work ceases to be a bore.

Postscript - summer 1974

The programme for economic development in China is to raise productivity for the whole working population by improving health and education, by raising the fertility of the soil, by innovations in technology (whether borrowed from the West or evolved at home) and by amassing an appropriate stock of equipment. This requires a high level of diligence and integrity in all lines of activity, while allowing only a modest rate of rise of the standard of life, so as to maintain the ratio of accumulation to consumption. All this is to be achieved with the goodwill of the people by appealing to political consciousness rather than by regimentation or the incentive of individual acquisitiveness.

This is an imaginative conception that has never hitherto been realised; small idealistic groups that contract out of modern commercial society usually contract out of modern productivity as well and aim at the 'simple life'. In China the aim is to preserve the morality of primitive communism while introducing all the complexity of high scientific technology in an integrated national state.

With such a programme, it is inevitable that there should always be a temptation, at every level, to take short cuts. Not all individuals are highly intelligent and perfectly well behaved; a responsible leader must often be tempted to resort to 'commandism' to bring the awkward workers into line or to resort to the bribery of money incentives to activate the sluggards. Recently, a new temptation has arisen — to slack off a little now that a high level of production has been reached. Moreover, in any large organisation there must be a chain of command, and it is only human for those high up the pyramid to feel that they are entitled to some privileges and to be tempted to use their position to secure them for themselves.

At each phase, as the programme develops, there is a right and left position on policy for the next step. In the economic sphere, the right stresses 'production' and the left, 'politics'. The left, of course, also aims to promote production. It is not against production, it is against taking short cuts. The left view is that by 'putting politics in command' a better economic foundation will be laid and that democratic, egalitarian methods will bring more production in the end than hierarchic, bureaucratic or purely technological methods of control.

In May 1972, when I was collecting the material for the original version of this booklet, reverberations of the ultra-left movement of the summer of 1967 and the spring of 1968 were still to be heard. For instance, in the first draft of my report, I made the generalisation, on the basis of what I was told in the particular places that I visited, that bonuses for plan-fulfilment had been completely abolished, but it appears that in other places they were still in use. Roland Berger reports that, towards the end of a discussion with members of the Revolutionary Committee of an engineering factory in Sian, in November 1972, a casual reference was made to the payment of bonuses. To raised eyebrows and the comment 'Shades of Liu Shao-chi?' came the response that these were not bonuses of the old type but were collective, each member receiving the same amount based upon the work team's production performance over a period of time. With the Sian experience in mind, he raised the question of bonus payments a few days later at a machine tool factory in Peking, to be met with a forceful rejection of any such unthinkable idea. Clearly, if there was a tendency towards a softer attitude to material incentives, it was not universal.

It has become clear from later Chinese comment and from personal observations during visits in spring and autumn 1973 and the spring of 1974 that, under the cover of criticising ultra-leftism, there was a swing to the right in some places and on the part of some cadres. The new campaign to criticise Confucian ideas (which are associated with the teaching of Lin Piao) is a swing the other way.

An important ingredient of the present movement is the attack on the Confucian notion that some are born to rule and others to labour. 'The superior man cannot be known in little matters; but he may be entrusted with great concerns. The small man may not be entrusted with great concerns but he may be known in little matters'. In terms of the operations of industry, this implies reliance upon an elite management and a sharp differentiation between cadres and workers in pay and in status.

On the philosophical plane, the argument is conducted in terms of the Marxian concept of the relation between the productive forces (roughly — physical conditions of production) and the relations of production (roughly — the pattern of attitudes, rights and duties within which work is carried out).

Mao Tse-tung has stated that 'when it is impossible for the productive forces to develop without a change in the relations of production, then the change in the relations of production plays the principal and decisive role.'

From statements at the Tenth Communist Party Congress (August 1973) we learn that, in the original draft of his report to the Ninth Congress in April 1969, Lin Piao, with Chen Po-ta as mentor, advanced the view that henceforward the main task was to 'develop production', implying that the necessary changes in productive *relations* had been successfully achieved by the Cultural Revolution. Lin Piao's draft was rejected. The report he actually delivered was prepared by the Central Committee and included a reference to 'the capitalist roaders in power (who) whipped up the evil counter-revolutionary wind of economism after failing in their scheme to suppress the revolution, on the pretext of "grasping production".'

The emphasis on technology at the expense of human relations, in Mao's view, does not in fact lead to faster economic growth. When the political consciousness of the people is not mobilised, administration has to rely on a privileged hierarchy of command, in the Soviet style, and on rigid bureaucratic rules. Then, since the political motivation for work flags, the administration has to fall back on 'economism' — appealing to individual monetary incentives.

A swing to the right had evidently not gone very far, but big-character posters which were appearing in some places in the summer of 1974 suggested that certain cadres were forgetting the verdict of the Cultural Revolution on the role of material incentives in the economy. Wang Hung-wen stated at the Tenth Party Congress:

> The working class, the poor and lower-middle peasants and the masses of working people are the masters of our country. They have the right to exercise revolutionary supervision over cadres of all ranks of our Party and state organs . . . However, there are still a small number of cadres, especially some leading cadres, who will not tolerate differing views of the masses inside and outside the Party. They even suppress criticism and retaliate, and it is quite serious in some individual cases. In handling problems among the people, Party discipline absolutely forbids such wrong practices as resorting to 'suppression if unable to persuade, and arrest if unable to suppress.'

It seems that reliance is being placed upon criticism from below to keep administration on the right path. A minor example of venting a complaint was cited above.* Now wider issues are being discussed. The movement shows the resolution of the workers, peasants and students to preserve and safeguard the 'socialist new-born things' achieved by the Cultural Revolution:

> Some comrades were not aware of the new things that emerged in the great proletarian Cultural Revolution; even if they were, they just supported them half-heartedly.
>
> (Report on Shenyang No. 1 Machine Tool Factory, March 1974)

Since the Tenth Congress, big-character posters have been appearing in large numbers in factories and communes where the workers and peasants consider that the gains of the Cultural Revolution are in jeopardy. At the same Shenyang No. 1 Machine Tool Factory, for example, it was reported that during March 1974, 1,500 big-character posters and more than 300 criticism meetings were held in the works. The seven standing committee members of the factory Party Committee participated in 23 criticism meetings and, in the presence of the workers, delivered 22 speeches in response to the criticisms.

On the rural front, a letter to all poor and lower-middle peasants in the province from the Hupeh Peasants' Congress held in December 1973, declared:

---

* See page 18.

The poor and lower-middle peasants must, under Party leadership, display the attitude of masters of the country and help and supervise cadres at all levels on the communes to carry out correctly the Party's line, principles and policies, take a firm class stand, take part in collective labour and run the communes democratically and diligently. We must actively support the work of the cadres and sincerely and skilfully put forward our views and criticisms of their shortcomings and mistakes.

A recurring theme in the campaign is to put politics not production in command. 'It seems,' said the Chayuan production team (Hunan) in criticism of the commune leadership, 'as if when we have output and income we have everything and we can cover up a hundred shameful things with just one good thing,' or, in the words of the workers of the Shanghai Port Bureau, 'be masters of the wharf, and not the slaves of tonnage.'

Many of the criticisms heard during the Cultural Revolution are being repeated in connection with methods of management, the role of material incentives in one form or another, factory rules and regulations, bloated administrations and the suppression of workers' technical innovations.

Recently, a woman worker in the Nantan county agricultural machinery repair factory, Kwangsi, had a letter published on the front page of the *Kwangsi Daily* in which she criticised the reversal of the decision during the Cultural Revolution to simplify the administration and reduce office personnel. The works leadership had transferred her for 'health reasons' from the workshop to the tool room to look after tools. 'It is shameful to prefer comfort,' she wrote, 'and most glorious to have the revolutionary spirit of arduous struggle. I don't want such care from the leadership.' She demanded her return to the workshop, and got it.

The reintroduction of material incentives, besides bonuses, sometimes takes the form of time off and assigning production quotas to individual workers. Railway workers in Harbin, Heilungkiang, complained that some leaders regarded material incentives as cure-alls. 'They look on the workers as money slaves instead of masters of enterprises.' Workers in a pharmaceutical plant in Huhehot, Inner Mongolia criticised the payment of an overtime allowance in addition to the regular overtime pay which drew from the secretary of the plant Party Committee the self-criticism that 'we became the slaves of money, corrupted the workers' thinking and followed the wrong line.' A poster put up by workers of the Chinghai gear works, Sining, criticised the payment of bonuses and granting time-off for the over-fulfilment of quotas and mentioned that some of them turned in their bonus money to the Youth League branches in their respective workshops. 'Some people attempted to use the method of going home immediately after completing a day's work to please us workers and make us happy,' stated a big-character poster written by railway workers in Liuchou, Kwangsi. 'However, we workers are not only not happy but are very indignant.'

There have been reports in the Western press of worse scandals being ventilated in posters. In places where there were sharp conflicts in the last stages of the Cultural Revolution, it is to be expected that problems should still remain to be sorted out.

The appeal, nowadays, is to public opinion and to the Party. The role of the PLA as a peacemaker seems to have come to an end. The representation of the PLA on lower-level revolutionary committees, also, has been further scaled down since 1972. It is rare to find any representation of the army on factory revolutionary committees today. The committees at commune and production brigade levels include, as they have done since the committees were originally formed, representatives of the people's militia but these are drawn from amongst their own members.

To conclude — in May 1972 I was observing the application, in the sphere of economic management, of the achievements of the Cultural Revolution in a relatively relaxed atmosphere without the tension and the extreme moral strenuousness that I had experienced in 1967. After the time of my visit, there seems to have been greater relaxation and some drift to the right. Now (July 1974) a return to the left is in full swing.

According to the philosophy of Mao Tse-tung, we should not look forward to some day when a final correct balance will be formed. 'One divides into two'. As every set of problems is solved, other problems emerge.

In the economic sphere, the problem is beginning to come up of the approach to affluence — what form should rising consumption take? At present, the principle is to raise the standard of life at the bottom while keeping it level at the top. Western observers sometimes ask, rather wistfully: when the Chinese become rich like us, will they not become just as selfish and corrupt as we are? One aim of the campaign to repudiate Confucius is precisely to prevent that from happening.

Cambridge
August, 1974. **Joan Robinson**